She Persisted

CORETTA SCOTT KING

—INSPIRED BY—

She Persisted

by Chelsea Clinton & Alexandra Boiger

· ·

CORETTA SCOTT KING

· ·

Written by
Kelly Starling Lyons

Interior illustrations by
Gillian Flint

PHILOMEL

PHILOMEL BOOKS
An imprint of Penguin Random House LLC, New York

First published in the United States of America by Philomel Books, an imprint of Penguin
Random House LLC, 2022

Text copyright © 2022 by Chelsea Clinton.
Illustrations copyright © 2022 by Alexandra Boiger.

Visit us online at penguinrandomhouse.com.

Library of Congress Cataloging-in-Publication Data is available.

Printed in the United States of America

HC ISBN 9780593353509
10 9 8 7 6 5 4 3 2 1
PB ISBN 9780593353523
10 9 8 7 6 5 4 3 2 1

WOR

Edited by Jill Santopolo and Talia Benamy.
Design by Ellice M. Lee.
Text set in LTC Kennerley.

∽ *For* ∾
my mom, grandmothers, aunts and
all of the sheroes whose shoulders I stand on.
Thank you for your commitment,
brilliance and love.

She
Persisted

Dear Reader,

As Sally Ride and Marian Wright Edelman both powerfully said, "You can't be what you can't see." When Sally said that, she meant that it was hard to dream of being an astronaut, like she was, or a doctor or an athlete or anything at all if you didn't see someone like you who already had lived that dream. She especially was talking about seeing women in jobs that historically were held by men.

I wrote the first *She Persisted* and the books that came after it because I wanted young girls—and children of all genders—to see women who worked hard to live their dreams. And I wanted all of us to see examples of persistence in the face of different challenges to help inspire us in our own lives.

I'm so thrilled now to partner with a sisterhood of writers to bring longer, more in-depth versions of stories of women's persistence and achievement to readers. I hope you enjoy these chapter books as much as I do and find them inspiring and empowering.

And remember: If anyone ever tells you no, if anyone ever says your voice isn't important or your dreams are too big, remember these women. They persisted and so should you.

Warmly,
Chelsea Clinton

CORETTA SCOTT KING

TABLE OF CONTENTS

....

CHAPTER I

Strong Roots

Named after her grandma Cora, Coretta Scott came into the world connected to a deep legacy of faith, bravery and belief in the importance of education. Everyone knew she was destined for something special. But no one—not even her parents or Coretta herself—could imagine that one day her voice and strength would inspire people around the world.

Born on April 27, 1927, at home in Perry

County, Alabama, Coretta was the child of Obadiah (Obie) Scott and Bernice McMurry Scott. They lived on family land in a house her father had built. Surrounded by the power of people who loved her, Coretta felt safe and protected. But outside the safety of their home, there were dangers everywhere.

In Alabama and throughout the South, segregation—racist laws that separated Black and white people—was the rule. Being Black meant you had to drink from "Colored" water fountains, go through back doors of businesses and restaurants and only be served after whites were. You were called hateful names and faced the danger of being hurt or killed because of the color of your skin. The weight of oppression was as thick as summer Alabama air. But the Scotts surrounded their kids with the winds of possibility.

In their proud Black community with family all around, there was a history of land ownership, hard-won and passed on. The Scotts knew land was a complicated issue full of injustice. The forced removal of the Muscogee people from their homelands and the terrible institution of slavery built wealth for some people while keeping others down. Decades later, many families who lived near Coretta's didn't own land and had little money. The unfairness broke Coretta's heart.

But being with her family brought her joy. She dreamed and explored as she played with her big sister Edythe, little brother, Obie Leonard, and cousins. She climbed trees, swung on tire swings, and wrestled boys. She was imaginative and strong—and proud of it.

"We were much better off when we created our own games rather than things you buy from the store," she said.

Sometimes Coretta would gaze in the mirror and wonder what she would be one day. She believed that God put everyone on Earth for a reason. What was her purpose?

Coretta found direction and inspiration in her heroes—her parents. Her mom had only finished fourth grade, and her dad one year of high school, but they were the smartest and most honorable people she knew. Her father owned his own truck and hauled lumber for a local sawmill company, and by making his own way in the world, he showed her what it meant to be independent and creative. Her mom, a seamstress and homemaker, instilled in Coretta and her siblings the value of faith, education, artistry and hard work.

Little Coretta helped her sister take care of the vegetables and feed the cows, chickens and hogs on their family farm. When she got older, Coretta and Edythe worked for a white farmer to help pay for their schooling. Unlike white students in their area, Black families had to pay for books. When the sun woke up, the Scott sisters started picking cotton with the heat beating on their backs. The days were long, tough and tiring. The sisters didn't finish until the sun went to bed. But Coretta put her all into it. She knew this work was a path to something more.

"You are just as good as anyone else," her mother would tell her. "You get an education and try to be somebody. Then you won't have to be kicked around by anybody, and you won't have to depend on anyone for your livelihood—not even on a man."

Sunshine or shower, Coretta walked with her siblings three miles to Crossroads, their crowded one-room school, where more than one hundred kids of different grades learned side by side. On the way, a bus filled with white students would pass them. Some days, the driver would splash mud or make clouds of dust fly into their eyes. Coretta knew the

school the white students were going to had a library, unlike her school, which didn't have as many books. White students got to attend school for nine months instead of seven like she and her friends did. Why did society treat her people that way?

Living in segregation brought daily pain and

heartbreak. Coretta couldn't stand having to crowd into the jam-packed balcony at the movie theater while white folks got to be comfortable on the main floor. She hated going to buy ice cream and only getting what flavors were left after the white customers chose. Racism hurt, but Coretta didn't let it shrink her spirit. Her parents taught her that.

Jealous of her dad's success, white men would stop him late at night to try to scare him. They would curse, pull out their guns. No matter what he faced, Obie Scott looked them in the eye. When things like this happened, Coretta's mom's words rang in her ears: "You are just as good as anyone else." Coretta remembered that and walked with her head held high.

CHAPTER 2

Gifted Voice

Freedom for Coretta came from her family, schooling and her special gift, singing. Growing up listening to her mom croon hymns and lullabies, Coretta found her voice too. At school and at Mount Tabor AME Zion Church, she sang solos. At home, she would sing along with her mom and sister or harmonize with records played on their Victrola. The world seemed to stand still as her voice soared to the stars.

At Crossroads, sixth grade was the high-
est grade offered. Coretta loved her teachers and
valued everything they taught her. But she longed
to learn more. Her parents had big dreams for

Coretta and her siblings. They wanted their kids to attend high school and college. How would they do it?

The Scotts paid a Black couple in Marion, a city about ten miles from their home, to let Coretta and Edythe live with them. That way, the sisters could go to Lincoln High School, a school that had been started after the Civil War to give Black students the education they had been denied before the war. There was a cost to attend—$4.50 per year per child. That was a lot in those days, but Coretta's parents covered it. They knew education opened doors to a better future. Coretta was thrilled. So many discoveries awaited.

At Lincoln, the teachers, Black and white, cared and did all they could to help students succeed. The fact that white teachers looked out for them made an impression on Coretta and filled her with hope. Maybe there were other white people who felt the same.

Coretta's favorite teacher, Miss Olive J. Williams, changed her life. She was a Black woman and graduate of Howard University—a historically Black college—and Columbia University, and she introduced Coretta to classical music and Black concert singers. Those became her new love.

Every year, the Lincoln chorus sang Handel's *Messiah*. It wasn't long before Coretta was singing solos just like she did back home. She took voice lessons with Miss Williams and learned as much as she could about famous Black singers like Marian Anderson and Paul Robeson. They not only moved people with their incredible voices but made a difference for civil rights, the

rights that all people have to be treated equally.

Coretta was discovering new sides of herself. She learned to play trumpet, flutophone and piano. She worked on her posture and pronunciation. She stood tall at concerts and sang with passion. Music gave her wings.

Though her life at school was full of joy, racism flourished outside the school walls. Students and teachers were harassed. People taunted them, called them slurs, blocked their path on the sidewalk.

Back home, every day brought new worries for her parents too. As her dad grew his business and went from owning one truck to three, the late-night threats from racist white men grew worse. One night Coretta and Edythe received awful news: Their family home had been set on fire. Coretta's parents and brother, Obie, escaped, but everything they owned burned in the blaze. Photos, keepsakes, clothes, the Victrola and the record collection that meant so much to Coretta were all gone.

Coretta grew up knowing that hate could strike at any time. But this was the day it came to their door. Her father didn't cry. He gave thanks that they were alive and prayed for the racists who lit the flames. Coretta was devastated, but his bravery and faith stuck with her. Those qualities would serve as an example throughout her life.

The family moved in with her grandfather, her mom's dad, until they saved enough to get another home. Not only did her dad accomplish that, he also eventually opened a lumber mill. He worked for himself and gave jobs to others. But before long, racists struck again and burned down his new business. Some people might have given up, but Coretta's father kept going. He worked, saved and believed, eventually opening up a grocery store.

Her mom showed Coretta how one person

could create change too. When Coretta was a junior, her dad transformed one of his trucks into a bus so Bernice Scott could become a bus driver, transporting Black students from Heiberger to Marion so more could attend high school. Coretta was able to move back home.

As Coretta progressed through school, her list of heroes grew—her parents, Miss Williams, Marian Anderson, Paul Robeson and others who created change, like First Lady Eleanor Roosevelt and college founder and leader Mary McLeod Bethune. Coretta respected and looked up to people who made a difference. Her purpose became clearer. She would use her voice to help the world shine.

CHAPTER 3

Determined to Succeed

Coretta's sister Edythe was the valedictorian—the top student—of her class at Lincoln and the first Black student to attend Antioch College in Yellow Springs, Ohio. Coretta followed in her footsteps as valedictorian and won a scholarship to Antioch too.

Ohio was in the north, and it was a state that didn't use a system of legal segregation, though some people and places in Northern states didn't welcome Black people either. Coretta hoped that leaving segregation would bring a new kind of freedom. Shy at first, Coretta soon found thoughtful teachers and warm and curious classmates. She made friends and devoted herself to studying elementary education and music.

She learned about different religions and nurtured her connection with God. At Antioch, she loved that giving back was stressed. "Be ashamed to die until you have won a victory for humanity" was a quote from an Antioch founder that echoed in her heart.

But after a while, Coretta recognized that discrimination—treating some people worse because of things like the color of their skin— wasn't always slurs and threats. Sometimes, white students asked questions that revealed negative

thoughts about the Black community. When
Coretta got upset, they would say that the bad
things that they were talking about didn't apply to
her, and that she was the exception. An insult to
her people was an insult to Coretta. It was wrong.

As part of her elementary education studies, she needed to spend two years teaching. She

taught at a school run by the college the first year. But when she applied to teach at a public school, the school board turned her down because she was Black. Coretta was qualified and ready. Why should her skin color mean that she couldn't get the job? Some students and professors rallied behind her, but her beloved school refused to take a stand.

Here was racism showing its hateful face again. Coretta ached, but she found community and strength in a group called the National Association for the Advancement of Colored People (NAACP), which worked to help Black people succeed and stood up for peace and equality.

Coretta continued to grow as a singer too, appearing in concerts around the area. Singing still sent her soaring, just as it did when she was a child.

At a national convention, she was overjoyed to be on the program with Paul Robeson. After hearing her sing, Robeson complimented and encouraged her. She always cherished that moment.

One of her favorite professors was head of the music department and the college's only Black faculty member. He suggested she continue her studies at a music conservatory, a school that specializes in music education. Coretta chose to attend the New England Conservatory in Boston. Rather than ask her dad to help with the fees, she applied for scholarships and prayed. No matter what, she'd earn what she needed. Coretta was a hard worker and determined to succeed.

At a stop on the train ride to Boston, she called her parents to check in and learned that she had won a grant covering her tuition. She could almost sing from excitement. Going to the conservatory was meant to be. Coretta took a job helping to clean the house where she stayed to cover her room and breakfast. She did other jobs to pay for extras. Some days, she only had peanut butter and graham crackers for dinner, but it was worth it.

Coretta immersed herself in studying voice and violin. Dating wasn't on her mind. But when a friend wanted to introduce her to a young doctoral student at Boston University named Martin Luther King Jr., she said okay. But she was still worried: He was a preacher, which made her wonder if they'd get along. What if he was stuffy and too serious?

When she met ML—that's what everyone called him—he was shorter than she imagined, but Coretta had to admit he had charm. As they ate at a local restaurant and talked, she found herself enjoying his company. When he drove her back home, ML made his intentions clear.

"He was looking for a wife. I wasn't looking for a husband. I resisted his overtures at first. I had to pray about it," she said.

Coretta wanted to marry and have a family one day, but she also dreamed of using her voice to make a difference. ML believed in the power of women, but wanted a wife who would be at home raising their children. Coretta wasn't sure that was a match for where she saw her life going. But as they dated, danced and joked, and discussed philosophy, religion and helping the Black community, a deep bond grew.

They fell in love and talked about peace and activism. ML shared his admiration for leaders like

Mahatma Gandhi, who showed how nonviolent resistance could be used to fight for change. Before Coretta knew it, their dreams intertwined.

The Rev. Martin Luther King Jr. and Coretta Scott married June 18, 1953, on her parents' front lawn. She wore a pastel blue wedding dress instead of the traditional white. Daddy King, ML's father and the pastor of Ebenezer Baptist Church in Atlanta, conducted the ceremony. At Coretta's request, he made an important change. He took the word *obey* out of the marriage vows.

The Kings returned to Boston to finish their schooling and then moved to Montgomery, Alabama, where Martin had his first congregation at Dexter Avenue Baptist Church. A new life had begun.

······························

CHAPTER 4

Fortified by Faith

In Montgomery, the Rev. Martin Luther King Jr. got to know his congregation. He believed all should be welcome at church and invited anyone he met to come. His warmth won him fans.

When people heard him preach, they were struck by how Rev. King explored what was happening around them. His sermons spoke of love for your fellow man, but also pushing for justice and

coping with racism. As he settled into his new role, Coretta did too.

As first lady of the church, she used her talents to help the choir become even better, joined committees and supported her husband's work. In the months that followed, Coretta was thrilled that their first child was on the way. But there was no escape from racism and hate.

Montgomery, where the Kings lived, had been the first capital of the Confederacy, which was the name for the Southern states that left the Union during the Civil War. It was a city full of the segregation and injustice of Coretta's youth. One of the countless wrongs was that Black passengers had to ride or stand at the back of buses. If a white person needed a seat and the white section was full, Black people had to give up seats in the back too.

That terrible law had been challenged many times. In one case, a fifteen-year-old Black girl named Claudette Colvin wouldn't give up her seat and was dragged off the bus and arrested. And then December 1, 1955, was a day like no other. Rosa Parks, a Black seamstress, rode home from work in the first row of the Blacks-only section. A white man demanded that she and the other passengers in her row get up so he could sit. Parks, the secretary of the local NAACP chapter, had enough and said no.

Police officers took her to jail. Dr. King—who had earned his doctorate degree after their move to Montgomery—and other preachers decided that the most powerful response would be a boycott of Montgomery buses—something a group of Black women had been talking about and building toward in an organization called the Women's Political Council. It quickly turned into a movement. People crammed into cars and rode in taxis. Many trudged miles to work by foot.

Days of the boycott turned into weeks and months. It made Coretta proud to see the empty buses and to see people standing together, but she knew that being a leader of the boycott made Dr. King a target.

Coretta pitched in with other women coordinating newspaper and TV interviews and volunteers. News spread around the world. They worked their phones at home, helping people who needed a ride. Threatening calls came day and night. People participating in the boycott faced abuse like hateful names, attacks and having urine thrown on them as they walked.

One day, shortly after the Kings' daughter Yolanda (nicknamed Yoki) was born, racists threatened to bomb their house if they didn't leave Montgomery. They stayed. Coretta was talking

with a church friend in her sitting room when the bomb landed on the front porch. They ran to the back of the house where little Yoki was in her bassinet. They were safe, but shattered glass, smoke and splintered wood filled the front of the house. What if they hadn't gotten away? Coretta was staring into the face of hate again. This time, she saw death.

Rather than scare her, the attack made Coretta stronger. She knew God had put her there for a reason that was even bigger than Montgomery. She and Dr. King had a calling.

"I realized that all my life I had been being prepared for this role," she said. "We were supposed to be there in Montgomery. It was a great feeling of satisfaction, because I realized that I had found my purpose."

When her parents and Dr. King's found out about the bombing, they wanted the young family to leave right away. It was too dangerous. Coretta and Dr. King stood their ground. They would stay and help fight for equality and freedom.

The costs included Dr. King and countless others going to jail, constant harassment and attacks, and people losing jobs. But they were fed up. It was time for change. Finally, after more than a year of boycotting, the Supreme Court ruled that Alabama's bus segregation wasn't lawful. They won.

"I was convinced that if I had not had a wife with the fortitude, strength and calmness of Coretta," Dr. King said. "I could not have stood up amid the ordeals and tensions surrounding the [Montgomery] movement."

CHAPTER 5

Freedom Fighter

On the first anniversary of the boycott, Coretta was the featured singer at a New York City benefit raising money for improving Montgomery. She couldn't believe she shared the program with stars like Harry Belafonte and Duke Ellington. When Coretta stepped onstage, dressed in an elegant gown, she let the struggle and strength of her people ring out in her voice. Spirituals, hymns and freedom songs mixed with the stories of the civil rights movement.

"My friends told me that the audience had been very receptive," she said, "but I knew it myself, because I could feel the warm, responsive love between us."

Raising a family and being part of the civil rights movement was tough, but Coretta was tougher. After the boycott, Dr. King's influence grew. Sometimes it seemed like he was gone more than he was home as he traveled around the country preaching and leading nonviolent protests. Coretta not only took care of their family, which eventually grew to four children—Yoki, Martin Luther III, Dexter and Bernice (Bunny)—but she also raised her voice. She spoke out against racism and discrimination and stood with her husband as often as possible.

Coretta traveled with Dr. King to Ghana and witnessed the birth of its freedom from British rule when the country flew its own flag for the first time. She traveled with him to India, singing on programs as he preached and walking in the footsteps of Gandhi. She was there for the unforgettable March on Washington, where Dr. King gave his famous "I Have a Dream" speech. More than 250,000 people gathered that day and millions more tuned in on the radio and TV. And she stood by his side the following year when he was awarded the Nobel Peace Prize.

Together, Coretta and Dr. King cheered victories like the 1964 Civil Rights Act and the Voting Rights Act, which were designed to protect Black people's rights in the US, and they supported each other through many struggles.

Coretta was Dr. King's wife and his intellectual and spiritual partner. She knew that every day their lives—and their children's—were on the line. Nonviolent resistance meant facing everything from name-calling to being beaten, jailed and even killed. But just like her parents taught her, Coretta believed that faith and standing up for freedom and justice could conquer anything. She walked with her head high and stared hate in the eye.

Coretta also came up with her own way to give back. As she thought about how much music meant to her and the civil rights movement, she remembered Paul Robeson, who would include storytelling in his performances, and she remembered the benefit that had been held on the first anniversary of the Montgomery bus boycott. What if she did similar concerts around the nation, sharing the Movement through story and song?

All of the steps along her journey had led to this moment. Singing with her mom and sister at home and at Mount Tabor AME Zion Church. Learning at Lincoln High School about how Marian Anderson and Paul Robeson had used their voices to make a difference. Seeing how music gave hope, inspiration and strength to people who were protesting for change. She named her idea Freedom Concerts. They would raise money for the Southern Christian Leadership Conference (SCLC), an important civil rights organization Dr. King led.

On November 15, 1964, she gave her first con-cert at The Town Hall in New York City. Dressed

in a stunning gown, her soprano voice carried the audience from the Montgomery bus boycott to the March on Washington. It was like a poem, diary and classical performance wrapped into one.

The response was immediate and electric. The press praised her mission to spread the word about the civil rights movement and raise money for the cause.

"The songs were almost all Negro spirituals, testaments of endurance and hope," said a *Newsweek* review. "Based as they are upon the Christian ethic of brotherhood and charity, they shed as much light on the struggle for civil rights now as they do on salvation later."

After performing at The Town Hall, Coretta did more than two dozen other Freedom Concerts and raised more than fifty thousand dollars. She used her voice in other ways too, speaking at rallies against the Vietnam War and encouraging her husband to do the same. Coretta was leading and making a difference just as she'd always dreamed.

CHAPTER 6

Legacy Builder

On the road to creating change, there was lots of pain beyond the attacks on their family and Dr. King being arrested and jailed. Children and adults committed to the Movement suffered and died. Coretta and Dr. King always knew that death could come at any time. Every time Dr. King was away and the phone rang, Coretta worried that it would be the news that would shatter her heart.

On April 4, 1968, came the day that Coretta dreaded. In Memphis to support striking sanitation workers, Dr. King was shot and killed on the balcony of the Lorraine Motel. He was only thirty-nine years old. Coretta didn't have much time to mourn. Along with her children, who needed a mother's comfort, she had a movement that longed for reassurance and hope. Just four days after Dr. King was killed, Coretta marched with Yoki, Martin Luther III, Dexter and a crowd of twenty thousand people and tried to finish his work.

"I come here today because I was impelled to come . . ." she said. "I ask the question, 'How many men must die before we can really have a free and true and peaceful society? How long will it take?' "

She spoke to the strength and resilience of

her family and drew on the power and unity of the Movement. Her bravery, grace and dedication touched people around the globe.

60 Minutes interviewed Coretta and her family the Christmas after Dr. King's assassination.

"In his death, there is hope for redemption," she said.

Coretta kept Dr. King's spirit alive for her family. He was present at the dinner table as she shared stories and reminded the kids what their father would say. He was there with her as she applauded their achievements. She wanted his legacy to continue for the world too.

She pushed for the government to make a national holiday to honor him. She envisioned a center that would represent all that he was and had given. She achieved both. Every year, we celebrate his birthday, Dr. Martin Luther King Jr. Day, as a national day of service. The Martin Luther King Jr. Center for Nonviolent Social Change in Atlanta attracts hundreds of thousands of visitors from around the world each year.

"Martin's message and his meaning were so powerful, and [I felt his spirit] needed to be continued," she said about founding the center. "I know that people's spirits live on, but I think in a very positive meaningful way that young people would know that influence was being continued."

People wanted to celebrate her too. The Coretta Scott King Book Award was founded in 1969 at the American Library Association. It was named after her to honor her "courage and determination to continue the work for peace and world brotherhood." Over the years, it grew to include multiple awards given in her name, including those recognizing illustrators. She became an honorary member of Alpha Kappa Alpha Sorority, Inc., the first Black Greek-letter sorority. Coretta continued to speak and sing throughout her life, protesting apartheid—a racist and unfair system that the government in South Africa used—and standing up for causes including voting rights, health care and the rights of all people to be free from unfairness and hate. "One of the reasons I wanted to join you today is to affirm my wholehearted

support of freedom from discrimination for lesbian and gay people," she said at the 1996 Atlanta Pride Festival. "I do so because I believe that all forms of persecution is wrong."

In countless ways, she carried out her and Dr. King's shared calling to promote peace, push for justice and show love for all humankind. Coretta traveled around the world, raising her voice and offering support to movements. She participated in historic events and protests. She wrote books and a syndicated newspaper column. Whenever Coretta could help, she was there.

Coretta, who some called the first lady of civil rights, died from cancer on January 30, 2006. In some states, flags were lowered to half-staff in honor of everything she had done. More than fourteen thousand people attended her funeral. Family, friends and fans came to say goodbye, along with presidents and stars like Oprah Winfrey and Maya Angelou, who held a special place in her heart.

Even today, her spirit and message live on. She was proud to be the wife of Dr. King, but she was a leader in her own right.

"I am not a ceremonial symbol," Coretta once said. "I am an activist. I didn't just emerge after Martin died—I was always there . . ."

HOW YOU CAN PERSIST

by Kelly Starling Lyons

Do you want to make a difference like Coretta Scott King? Here are some ways to get started:

1. Stay focused, learn as much as you can and work hard. Throughout her life, Coretta Scott King put her all into everything she did. That's how she became a leader.

2. Unite with others for a common cause. When people work together to make a difference, they can accomplish anything.

3. Be inspired by your heroes. Think about the people who make you proud, whose accomplishments make you dream big, whose courage gives you strength. Think about them when you need encouragement. They achieved success. You can too.

4. Hold on to hope and faith. No matter how tough times get, there's always good that can come and beauty that can grow. Believe that with all your heart.

5. Treat everyone with kindness. Tell an adult if you see someone being racist

toward someone else. Our country
is full of people from different races,
religions and backgrounds. That is our
strength.

6. Each of us has talents. Use your gifts
to make our world better. Dig deep and
find ways to give back. You can create
change just like Coretta Scott King.

Acknowledgments

When I saw the beautiful cover for this book, I was reminded of the importance of giving people their flowers. Mrs. Coretta Scott King was a visionary, leader, freedom fighter and humanitarian whose contributions lift us all. It was such an honor to write about her for the She Persisted series. The women of the civil rights movement deserve to be celebrated. Mrs. King's courage and conviction fill me with pride. I hope that children will be inspired by her life and follow her example of showing love, using their gifts to make a difference and standing up for what they believe.

Thank you to Chelsea Clinton for creating the She Persisted collection of books. What a blessing to have a literary sisterhood dedicated to lifting up women who have changed our world for the better. Thank you to editors Jill Santopolo and Talia Benamy for choosing me for this project and for their insightful guidance. I also applaud illustrators Alexandra Boiger and Gillian Flint, the entire Philomel team and my agent, Caryn Wiseman. This book would not be possible without them.

While I'm passing out flowers, let me share some with my family. Always in my corner, they remind me to write from the heart and stand tall. Special shout-outs to my mom, children, Brown Bookshelf buddies, Novelette sisters, Quint fam, sorors and friends, including Traci Sorell, who offered important feedback.

I loved learning about the people who helped shape Mrs. Coretta Scott King's amazing life. It made me reflect on the many who have poured into me. I'd like to end with a bouquet of thank-yous to a few teachers and mentors who put me on this path—Wade Hudson and Cheryl Willis Hudson, Lerone Bennett Jr., Basil Phillips and Dr. Janis Mayes.

❧ References ❧

BOOKS
....

Bagley, Edythe Scott, and Joe Hilley. *Desert Rose: The Life and Legacy of Coretta Scott King*. Tuscaloosa, AL: University of Alabama Press, 2012.

Herman, Gail. *Who Was Coretta Scott King?* New York: Penguin Workshop, 2017.

King, Coretta Scott. *My Life with Martin Luther King, Jr.* New York: Holt, Rinehart and Winston, 1969.

King, Coretta Scott, and Rev. Dr. Barbara
Reynolds. *My Life, My Love, My Legacy*.
New York: Henry Holt & Company, 2017.

Shange, Ntozake. *Coretta Scott*. New York:
Katherine Tegen Books, 2009.

ARTICLES

"Montgomery Bus Boycott." The Martin
Luther King, Jr. Research and Education
Institute, Stanford University. https:
//kinginstitute.stanford.edu/encyclopedia
/montgomery-bus-boycott.

Theoharis, Jeanne. "I am not a symbol, I am an
activist: the untold story of Coretta Scott
King." *The Guardian*. February 3, 2018. https:

//www.theguardian.com/world/2018/feb/03
/coretta-scott-king-extract.

DOCUMENTS

CNN. "Coretta Scott King Funeral Program."
i.a.cnn.net/cnn/2006/images/02/07/scott
_funeral_program.pdf.

Jones, Randye L. "The Legacy of Coretta Scott
King: A Gracious Voice and Divine Spirit."
artofthenegrospiritual.com/research
/CorettaScottKingLecture041611.pdf.

The Town Hall. "Freedom Concert Program."
thetownhall.org/history.

VIDEOS

60 Minutes. "1968 Interview with MLK's Family."
YouTube. April 4, 2018. youtube
.com/watch?v=76sUnyO0ooM.

ABC News. "April 8, 1968: Memphis March
Honors MLK." YouTube. January 15, 2010.
youtube.com/watch?v=Ya2ooRFWZkk.

Academy of Achievement. "Coretta Scott King,
Academy Class of 1997, Full Interview."
YouTube. July 30, 2016. youtube.com
/watch?v=7DX5pyvAXz0.

E. F. T. V. "1996 Atlanta Gay Pride Festival Speech
by Coretta Scott King." YouTube. October 7,
2009. youtube.com/watch?v=bHm8djZqTzk.

Interview with Coretta Scott King, conducted by Blackside, Inc. on November 21, 1988, for *Eyes on the Prize II: America at the Racial Crossroads 1965 to 1985*. Washington University Libraries, Film and Media Archive, Henry Hampton Collection. http://digital.wustl.edu/cgi/t/text /text-idx?c=eop;cc=eop;rgn=main;view=text; idno=kin5427.0224.089.

visionaryproject. "Coretta Scott King: My Childhood as a Tomboy / Growing into a Lady." YouTube. March 22, 2010. youtube.com /watch?v=8FlFKG5p31k.

visionaryproject. "Coretta Scott King: My Singing Career." YouTube. March 22, 2010. youtube.com /watch?v=QAS8EisdAGI.

KELLY STARLING LYONS is a founding member of the Brown Bookshelf, teaching artist and award-winning children's book author. Her mission is to center Black heroes, celebrate family, friendship and heritage and show all kids the storyteller they hold inside. Many of her books have won accolades including a Caldecott Honor for *Going Down Home with Daddy*, Geisel Honor for *Ty's Travels: Zip, Zoom*, Christopher Award for *Tiara's Hat Parade*, Bank Street Best list for *Sing a Song: How Lift "Every Voice & Sing" Inspired Generations* and Junior Library Guild selection for *Dream Builder: The Story of Architect Philip Freelon*. She's also the author of the popular Jada Jones chapter book series.

You can visit Kelly online at
kellystarlinglyons.com
or follow her on Twitter
@kelstarly

GILLIAN FLINT has worked as a professional illustrator since earning an animation and illustration degree in 2003. Her work has since been published in the UK, USA and Australia. In her spare time, Gillian enjoys reading, spending time with her family and puttering about in the garden on sunny days. She lives in the northwest of England.

You can visit Gillian Flint online at
gillianflint.com
or follow her on Twitter
@GillianFlint
and on Instagram
@gillianflint_illustration

CHELSEA CLINTON is the author of the #1 *New York Times* bestseller *She Persisted: 13 American Women Who Changed the World*; *She Persisted Around the World: 13 Women Who Changed History*; *She Persisted in Sports: American Olympians Who Changed the Game*; *Don't Let Them Disappear: 12 Endangered Species Across the Globe*; *It's Your World: Get Informed, Get Inspired & Get Going!*; *Start Now!: You Can Make a Difference*; with Hillary Clinton, *Grandma's Gardens* and *Gutsy Women*; and, with Devi Sridhar, *Governing Global Health: Who Runs the World and Why?* She is also the Vice Chair of the Clinton Foundation, where she works on many initiatives, including those that help empower the next generation of leaders. She lives in New York City with her husband, Marc, their children and their dog, Soren.

You can follow Chelsea Clinton on Twitter
@ChelseaClinton
or on Facebook at
facebook.com/chelseaclinton

ALEXANDRA BOIGER has illustrated nearly twenty picture books, including the She Persisted books by Chelsea Clinton; the popular Tallulah series by Marilyn Singer; and the Max and Marla books, which she also wrote. Originally from Munich, Germany, she now lives outside of San Francisco, California, with her husband, Andrea, daughter, Vanessa, and two cats, Luiso and Winter.

You can visit Alexandra Boiger online at
alexandraboiger.com
or follow her on Instagram
@alexandra_boiger

Read about more inspiring women in the

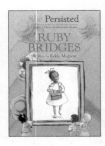

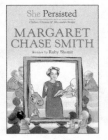

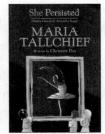

She Persisted series!

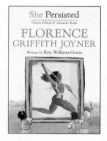

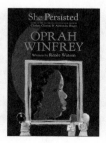